"Faith is the first factor in a life devoted to service.
Without it, nothing is possible.
With it, nothing is impossible."

Dr. Mary McLeod Bethune
~Founder of Bethune Cookman University~

BE CALM! BE STEADFAST! BE COURAGEOUS!
Mustard Seed Faith

"Your faith will carry you to places that your eyes can't see– walk by faith."

Tressan Thompson

Mustard Seed Faith. Copyright © 2018. Tressan Thompson. All Rights Reserved.

Printed in the United States of America.

No portion of this book may be reproduced, stored in a retrieval system, or transmitted in any form or by any means, except for brief quotations in printed reviews, without the prior written permission of Tressan Thompson and DayeLight Publishers.

Unless otherwise indicated, all scripture quotations are taken from the King James Version.

Book Cover Design by HCP Book Publishing

ISBN: 978-1-949343-24-3

TABLE OF CONTENTS

Acknowledgments vii
   Contributors viii

Behind the Novel: "Walk by Faith, Not by Sight" ... ix

Prologue xi

Introduction... 1

Chapter 1
   The Power of Prayer 3

Chapter 2
   The Tight Place 17

Chapter 3
   Bitten but Not Beaten 25

A Letter to My Readers..37

Conclusion	39
When You Need Motivation	41
Famous Motivational Stories	47
Elephant Rope	47
Lulu Roman's Story	48
The Obstacle in Our Path	50
Dedication to Mama	53

Acknowledgments

Special thanks to my wonderful editors, Cassandra Everett and Crystal Daye, for showing me a brighter light and helping me to provide a tighter story for this book.

Thanks to my sisters and my cousin, Tiffany, for pumping me to continue with this book.

Thanks to my other half, who was always there taking care of me and my mental health throughout the time of writing and promoting this book.

I want to thank God because without Him, my dreams wouldn't have become a reality. Far too often, we forget Him in our doings, not realizing that all things happen because of Him. With God everything is possible.... every single thing.

I want to thank my mother who is my rock, my strength and my armour. My mother is truly a blessing in my life. Just her mere presence propels me to go on and continue to fight the fight. I just want to thank her for molding me into the vessel of honor that I am today. I am who I am because of her fervent prayers.

Contributors

A huge thanks to Mr. Phillip Williams for his contributions to this book, along with Simone Campbell.

Time wouldn't allow me to thank everyone who has always been there for me, but I appreciate you all.

Behind the Novel: "Walk by Faith, Not by Sight"

This book was inspired by a young lady, Cherish Walker, who grew up in a local community called Barry Hill. As a child, she was abandoned by her father, and she is now using his absence as a motivational tool to conquer all the fears that might hinder her from becoming a leading light.

It was her childhood dream to attend college to become a teacher, but she had some challenges. She overcame most of them, but there were now higher mountains to climb. Would she lose faith, or would she continue climbing?

Prologue

As I peered into the classroom, I looked around in disbelief. I thought to myself, *"Am I really here?"* A tear trickled down my cheek, and I swallowed hard. I was lost for words. I was humbled yet honored.

Finally, I was about to be in a room filled with fellow college colleagues. I looked across the room, and I couldn't be more pleased. All that I went through wasn't in vain. I was finally in college because I had the courage to step off the ledge, I endured the pain, I stuck with God, and I had a *Mustard Seed Faith*.

Introduction

Have you ever secretly been in a tight situation? You continuously smile around people, and they have no idea what is going on in your head?

Have you ever gotten tired of being in the same place? You wonder if you should give up on your dreams or not?

You are having the same argument with the same husband? You are going through the same pattern daily? You are putting up with the same craziness at work, at home, or at school?

It's not forever!

You have prayed, cried all the tears, and tried all you could. You may feel as if God is against you but---

Nothing is against you!

Your situations are symbolic to mountains. These mountains won't hurt you. In your climbing God will mould you. Yes, you may break, but He will mend you. Your mountains will change you into a better person.

It had to happen!

Everything you go through is for a reason. You might not see it now but watch out for later days.

Do not give up!

This novel will reassure readers to never lose their faith and hope in whatever they believe in. This is a restoration of faith. Hold on a little longer and remember where and why you started. As long as you have faith and have God on your side, you can fulfill your dreams. I hope readers will enjoy *Mustard Seed Faith* as much as I enjoyed writing it.

WHATEVER YOU DO, DO NOT LOSE FAITH!

CHAPTER 1

The Power of Prayer

We waited for him, but he never showed up.

I was approximately two years old when my father disappeared from my life. My father broke my heart before anyone else had the chance to. He left a hole in my heart. There was emptiness, a hollow, because like every average child, I wanted to grow with him. He was supposed to see me making my first step, run around with me, carry me to my bed at night, help me to be strong, and show me all the fatherly qualities that a daughter needs while growing up.

My mother had to do it all on her own, and I had to learn the hard way that life goes on. She was a woman of brown complexion, stout, and short in height. She was only twenty-four years of age when she gave birth to me. After my father's departure, I wanted him to come back and sweep my mother off her feet, but he didn't.

There was no contact.

There was no money.

We had to move in with my grandmother, my cousin, Tashi, and my two other siblings, Lorna and Janice. Tashi was two years old; Janice was four years old, and Lorna was seven. My grandmother was a middle-aged woman; strong, confident, and hardworking yet ferocious and insolent.

My grandmother resided in a small community called Barry Hill. We stayed in a house with only two rooms. One was used as the bedroom, and the other was used as the kitchen. My grandmother's house was made with bamboo, decorated with flour and newspaper as the wallpaper. The roof was made with thatch, the floor was red dirt, and a sheet of zinc was used as the door. We had no electricity; therefore, we used a little lamp as our source of light. When it was cold, we wrapped sheets around the bamboo to prevent us from catching a cold. When it was raining, we used basins to collect water because of the leakage from the roof.

We stayed with my grandmother for a long time. During that time, we went through bitter-sweet moments. My grandmother, being an insolent but rather sweet woman, would wake up most mornings singing her

Christian songs, for example, *"Meet Me by the River,"* or we would wake up to the sweet aroma of cinnamon cornmeal porridge. At night, she would tell us famous Anancy stories, for example, *Anancy and Beetle Bug* and *Anancy in the Hotel*. My favorite one was *Anancy and the Cow*.

Other nights were completely different. Sometimes it felt as if grandmother wanted us to leave. She said no words, but her actions were graceless toward us. We would hear her hissing her teeth continuously and making movements on the bed while my mother and I listened quietly on the red dirt floor. When the following morning came, it was chaotic. She was a vendor at Moore Town Primary and Junior High, so she had to wake up very early. She arose with excessively loud singing, and it wasn't a gospel song; it was profanity at its highest peak. She would open her *"door"* loudly or rattle her *lovely food pots* on the plate stand formally known to Jamaicans as the *"kata."* She would quarrel about who was supposed to wash the sheets that we used on her red dirt floor and who was being lazy for not bringing the plates to the nearby river to wash. This disgusting noise was the alarm clock for my cousin and two sisters because they had to get up for school. Janice was attending basic school, and Lorna was attending primary school.

Before they left for school, they had to go to a nearby spring with their containers to collect water and take a bath. I watched them every morning going through this same routine with their tiresome faces. Most times, I could tell that they didn't want to go by their red-rimmed looking eyes and how they dragged their feet. Each morning when they went out, my mother prayed for them with tears in her eyes because she knew that for the entire or nearly most of the day, they would be hungry. Fortunately, on Tuesdays and Thursdays, they could afford the school buns and drinks. Often, they brought home a bag or two for the family.

My mother didn't like the situation, so she resorted to selling goods around the community, and she never ceased praying. She had three children with no support from their father. What better choice was there than to pray? My mother did her best. She tried to keep us tight and close. From a very tender age, my mother brought us to church every Sunday, and she taught us how to read our Bibles and pray. She told us to pray when things are good and especially when things are going bad because prayer makes a difference. She taught us these lines from the Bible, *"Trust in the Lord with all thine heart and lean not to thy own understanding. In all thy doings acknowledge him and he shall direct thy path."* Those words never left our lips, and even when we prayed before breakfast, lunch, or dinner, we would recite those words.

Even though life wasn't great for us, Mommy made us happy. She didn't only limit us to church. We loved to accompany her on Saturday morning to sell her goods, and sometimes she allowed us to go to a nearby farm with our neighbor, Marshawn. We loved Marshawn because we could watch television at his house and we went to birthday parties and fun days with him. You would see us in each other's clothing, but we were happy just the same. Our happiness was at its peak when it was Christmas time. We could now go to more parties and fun days, and we had the opportunity to play with new toys and go on rides.

In contrast, when other families sat around tables eating their various meals and drinks, we sat on our red dirt floor eating crackers and milo. We were very grateful because it was our favorite. Our mother taught us that we should always be grateful for what we have. However, when everyone else went to bed, my siblings and I would listen to the combustion around us. We fell asleep speaking of our dreams and aspiration of what we would want our Christmas to be like. I had hope in everything we spoke about. I knew that our dreams would one day become a reality.

The situation was getting unbearable, so my mother got a job in the nearby district called Windsor on a banana farm, where I accompanied her every day to help her out. She met my future stepfather on that farm, and she planned to move in with him. Unfortunately, she had to leave my two sisters behind with my grandmother because my stepfather didn't have much room. We moved early one Tuesday morning. As we were leaving that morning, my siblings ran behind us with tears running down their cheeks. My mother turned to look back at them. Her lips were pressed together in distress and it took her two minutes to speak. When she spoke, it was a cracked voice, but she promised them that she would return soon. She knew in her heart that it would take some time, but she wanted to comfort them even though she didn't want to leave them behind with my grandmother. My mother made it her point of duty to visit them every weekend to make sure they were okay. Even though my grandmother was such a crazy woman, she still took care of them.

My stepfather was a rough looking farmer who sold goods at Coronation Market in Kingston, and from time to time, my mother and I went along with him. Sometimes my mother and I went alone because my stepfather had to take care of his farm back home. I often looked upon my mother's beautiful face and could see that she was broken and tired. She wanted to rest but she couldn't. She had to keep going even when I fell asleep on the market truck.

My mother was strong. While at the market, I would watch her carrying bunches of bananas on her head while having other fruits in her hand. *Was she Goliath?* I had no idea, but all I knew was that she possessed the strength of a lioness. I saw my mother as a person who never gave up. It was in those moments that she became my role model. I was only six when I fell in love with her strength. She was tired, and it was as if she was being paid to not give up. I knew that most times when she closed her eyes on the truck, she was praying, and her prayers were answered because we came home safe every night. Even when we didn't make enough money, our life being spared was just enough. When she came home, she was extremely tired. When she fell asleep, I looked at her motionless body lying down, and I thought, *"Things will be okay, Mommy. It will get better."* My mother wasn't qualified to work in any bank or supermarket because her education was hindered by an early pregnancy and her lack of resources. Therefore, she had no other choice but to settle for patchiness.

While living with my stepfather, I welcomed my little brother, Oshane, into this world but things were still not better for us. In 2006, when most things were modernized, we weren't. We were destitute, yet happy. Each morning before we went to school, we prayed, and our mother packed our lunches in paper bags and placed them in our schoolbags along with our little blue Bibles. We didn't have much, but I was sure that our lunches were packed with things that others didn't have. My mother plastered our bread with grace, our juice was made with fervent prayers, and our paper bags were folded with guidance. However, some mornings were different. We only went with our bus fares and no breakfast. Our parents sent us because they didn't get an education, so they worked hard to ensure that we had one. On the mornings we didn't have any breakfast, we certainly didn't leave home without praying. My mother built a prayer life with us because she told us prayer changes everything.

My brother and I were clever. When we had more money than usual, we saved towards buying small gifts for our parents. My brother bought for my mother, and I bought for my stepfather. I had to appreciate my stepfather because he stepped in where my father fell short. He showed me love, but there was still this emptiness in my heart. I still wanted my father to be around. I really wanted to grow with my real father, but at the end of the day, I couldn't be ungrateful.

While others had their bath in bathrooms under their exquisite showers, we used the famous *"Dons River"* as our magnificent bathroom, where we swam as we liked, splashed loudly, and made sounds. We woke up at approximately six in the morning and took long strolls to take a bath. When we were at school, we would hear students saying, *"The shower wasn't even working this morning"* or *"No water was coming from the pipe in the face basin."* We had no idea what those were, so we had to keep quiet because we definitely couldn't just play along. My mother taught us to be true to ourselves. The only thing we knew was to dip our toothbrush in the cold river water and brush our teeth. Some mornings were difficult, especially when it was cold. We hid most of those mornings and told our parents that we already went. The cold was excruciating.

One morning, we lost track of time and got the beating of our lives. We were down by the river role-playing and talking about what we wanted to be in the future. We made a small shower down there, and the water would run down our backs. We didn't want to miss out on anything, and we sure didn't miss out on any punishment that morning. We went to school in tears for being disobedient and tardy. My mother believed in discipline and punctuality.

Our kitchen was on the outside. When the rain fell, it was hard for us. Either there would be no dinner, or my mother would take the cooking out on our veranda. She prepared our meal on a wood fire. Sometimes we had to borrow the ingredients needed to prepare dinner. We had to borrow an iron to press our uniforms for school. My family didn't even have a television.

One night, we went to sit outside our neighbor's house to watch the *School Challenge Quiz*. In the midst of watching, I saw one of them using her toes to push the door, so we could no longer see. We were sitting on the veranda. My brother and I felt utterly disrespected. We got up and went home. We didn't tell our parents because we knew how they would feel. Enough was already going on. We had to keep that one to ourselves.

Most times at school, I was being jeered by fellow *"friends"* that my house was made out of board and I was poor. I cried on the inside, but no one saw the real tears. I knew things wouldn't always be like that.

Additionally, when the rain fell at school, we would take off our school shoes, and go home barefooted to preserve our shoes. If we didn't take care of them, our little asses were going to be on fire and we would have to sit out that entire term.

There were nights when my brother and I came home tired as a result of netball and football practices with nothing to eat. We had to drink tea or water and go straight to bed. However, when there was food, there was no electricity because there was no money to pay the bills. Each night, we prayed because we didn't want to give up.

At school, we hardly went on trips like other students, and even when we did, we took turns and shared what happened and told each other about all the great buildings, toys, etc. that we saw. Our favorite spot was Manor Park in Kingston because we loved eating Kentucky Fried Chicken.

Despite all the challenges, we were having good times. Whenever we heard the lines *"Riddle me this, riddle me that,"* joy filled our minds and bodies because we knew my stepfather was about to tease us with questions that would have us rolling on the floor with laughter. The greatest thing was that if we answered correctly, we got sweets and a chance to ride on his back. Also, we loved waiting up for him to come from the market because he always brought home toys and fried chicken for us.

We loved going to the river on Saturdays to play with our friends. When we completed our homework, we had the entire day for ourselves. We caught fish and fried them for our lunch, and then we swam for the rest of the day. Some Saturdays we went to the farm with my parents and had the time of our lives because each of us got to ride my stepfather's donkey.

We were also excelling at school, and I believe it was because of our prayer life. Additionally, while our parents were at the farm, we stayed home and studied. We wanted to get all our work done. My brother was the captain of both the cricket and football teams. I was a member of the netball team, most outstanding debater, excelling in Mathematics and English competitions, and a member of the 2008 KFC Quiz Show team. These accomplishments made my mother and my stepfather work even harder for us.

At nights, we continued to pray for even better days, and my mother continually gave us words of encouragement to never give up. I can remember reading a note in my brother's Bible, *"Lord, please help me to become a great cricketer."* I knew God saw that, but it wasn't just writing, as my brother continued to work toward it.

By the time I was 12, I had another brother. Now I fully understood life and continued to have faith. However, I still wasn't accustomed to my biological father. I heard rumors that he had three other children, and my mother now wanted me to visit him. My mother had a big heart, but I didn't. She didn't know the bitterness that was in my heart for my father. However, she forced me to visit him to get money to attend school, and I had to go even though I was reluctant.

When I went to stay with him, it was very uncomfortable because I wasn't acquainted with him and he hardly gave me any attention. When he was at the house, I sat and looked at him without anyone noticing. I couldn't think of him in any way other than the man who bailed on me when I was just a baby. At nights, I watched him with his big, strong arms carrying my smaller sibling to her little bed and I couldn't be more uncomfortable. I was dying to leave. When I left on Monday morning for school, he sent me to my mother with notes and no money saying that he had nothing. This made me even more furious. *Couldn't he just tell me that? Did he think that I couldn't read?*

The more I grew, the more I promised myself that I would work harder for my mother. I didn't understand why my father didn't care for me in ways that a father should and even though the situation made me sad, I had to pray that things would get better.

Of course I had nothing but love for my other siblings, but for him, I made up my mind to make him regret the days that he didn't take care of me and for abandoning me when I needed him most. I didn't want to be bitter. It was not healthy for a young girl to have so much hatred, but I needed an explanation for why I was abandoned as a child; I didn't get one.

The Grade Six Achievement Test was now approaching, and I planned on using my father's absence and my everyday struggles as my motivation. Every night, I could hear my mother praying that I would excel. I studied well because I didn't want to let her down. I knew that with God's grace, I would move on to my dream school.

At that time, my grandmother was in the hospital battling with a stomach problem. Throughout that time, I realized that prayer was mobile. It was fast. My mother and I prayed fanatically about my grandmother's health, and our prayer traveled to the hospital because she told us at the time of her recovery that she felt in her body that, *"Somebody was praying for her."*

Our faith helped her recover, and it was that same faith that helped me pass for Titchfield High School. That was a moment I wished my father would show up so that he could see what was happening. He wasn't around to help, but I needed his presence. He wasn't there, so I presumed he wasn't proud of me.

Nevertheless, without his help and with all that my family was going through, I came out as a victor. I was the honoured valedictorian at my school's graduation, and I won a school scholarship. I was a champion because of my mother's prayers. With all those accomplishments, I was ready for a new beginning in high school, and great things awaited me because I knew that my mother would never stop praying.

I dare you to pray!

CHAPTER 2

The Tight Place

Our smiles broadened as we left for school in September, 2008. We wore our new uniforms and footwear received from the Food for the Poor organization. Nobody knew that but us, and we were very proud, proud to be going to school.

Mommy told us, *"Someone is always going through something worse than you are. Hold your head high, never give up, and remember where you are coming from."*

Those words diffused and disseminated inside my brain and body. I loved my mother so much because she never fell short, especially with her unconditional love for her children. She reminded us every day of who we are, prayed with us, and encouraged us to pray.

She said, *"PUSH: P is for Pray, U is for Until, S is for Something, and H is for Happens; Pray Until Something Happens."*

When I entered the 7th grade, my brother was still in primary school, and my two sisters had come to join us in Windsor. It hurt so much when we were separated, so now that we were together, I was elated.

I entered high school with the mentality to work hard and keep my eyes on the prize. I had to remember my core, my central point.

My days went well, and things were looking up for my family because we now owned a television. We watched television every night. Our favorite cartoon was *Hey Arnold*, and we watched it every night until it was time for bed.

Then things went downhill. My stepfather wasn't making enough money at the market, and my mother was laid off from the banana farm. I saw God blessing our neighbor, which meant that God was in the neighborhood, so I figured He would bless us next. But I was so wrong! It felt as if each time good presented itself, the bad came up from nowhere. I felt like God wasn't listening to our needs and our prayers were in vain. I knew that everything happens according to God's timing, but I was getting impatient, and I was losing faith.

Throughout that time, we somehow managed to attend school, but we had to take turns. Some days I attended, and then my brother, Oshane, and then my sibling, Janice. We were assertive, so when we went back to school, we caught up on what we lost.

When the term ended, I came second in my class. My brother passed for Port Antonio High, and my sister graduated with her certificate from the same institution. That was in the year 2010. In the same year, I became a Christian. I knew everything was going wrong, so I planned on handing it all to Jesus. What other choice did I have? After all, He was the only one I knew who could fix my problems. Well, that is what my mother taught me.

My Christian journey went great for an entire year until I went to the ninth grade. So many things were still happening at home, and like every other teenager, I encountered peer pressure. I made friends who were unorthodox. Therefore, my whole attitude changed, and I forgot about the promise I made to God and myself. I started being tardy, not attending classes, making amendments to my uniform, and not doing assignments. I totally forgot about my dreams and aspirations, and it was evident because I fell back in my class. I became reckless, and it got even worse in the tenth grade. Of course, my mother didn't know about this, and I didn't want her to know. I knew I was off track and even if I wanted to get back on track, I couldn't. I was going at a rapid speed. It felt like I was driving with Paul Walker.

I clung to my friends to escape from reality. My friends were my medicine. At school, everyone thought I had it all under control. They thought I was an average kid because I hid it all under a smile. I was really losing it, but I thought that a smile and my clique was all I needed to fit in. I ran from reality. I tried to escape it so hard, but I couldn't because each evening I returned to the troubles back home. The troubles back home were one of the many things that brought me back to reality.

One evening when I came home, I met everyone on the veranda sitting in darkness. My stepfather sat at one corner with his head in his hands, while my other siblings sat staring out of space as if they were oblivious. My mother was nowhere to be found. When I went into the house, I heard her in her room. She was in the room on her knees crying and praying. When she was through, she told me that we would be out of electricity for some days because they had no money. My eyes were filled with tears. I was hit with a stroke of lightning. I realized that I needed to get my life together before it was too late. I needed to work hard for my mother to be okay. I had to return to my center to remind myself of who I was and believe in myself again. I had to remind myself of why I started because I would soon sit my Caribbean Examination Councils external exams. I knew I couldn't approach those exams with my present type of behavior and mindset.

I was recommended for all my subjects, which I had to pass for my mother to be proud. It came to a point where I had to be strong because I had no other option. I realized that if you don't have a place that you can go back to and recalibrate yourself, you won't know what you think or how you feel or who you are because you have lost your center. If you lose your center, you lose yourself.

Feeling like a giant refreshed with new wine, I went on to the 11th grade. It was now clear to me that I had to be meticulous in whatever I was doing. I prayed without ceasing and my faith enlarged; therefore, I treated every day like it was my last. I studied hard and was more involved in activities. Was it too late? No, it wasn't. Time was going, and I went with it.

Eleventh grade went well until it was time to pay for my exams. My two younger brothers were also in school, and my two sisters were now without a job. I prayed along with my mother and decided to talk with my deadbeat, traitor of a father again. I knew that at some point, I had to forgive him and move on. That was probably the moment to do so.

My mother heard rumors that he was overseas, which turned out to be true. She got his number and called him but there was no response. I thought about giving up, but that wasn't the way I was raised. I continued praying and waited. I wasn't planning on giving up on school. I continued to study, and there was no doubt in my mind that God would come through for me.

Countless nights I would hear my mother praying and asking God for resources to pay for my subjects. We had no money, but I could imagine how she begged God to push this through for her. My mother taught us how to pray fervently. She said, *"Pray like there is no tomorrow, and when you do, do so with faith. Faith is the premise that unlocks everything. Don't worry about your feelings. Your feelings don't know your future."*

A couple days passed, and we sat together talking about our next move. Our conversation was interrupted by a phone call from the Food for the Poor organization. They said that they were going to pay for my exams. Tears fell down my mother's cheeks while I sat down in disbelief. It had to be God. It proved to me that God doesn't get you into anything that He can't take you out of. Once He brings you to it, He will take you out of it. Prayer works, even when everything else fails.

God doesn't give a man more than he can bear, so He handled it all. I was happy, and I could now fully prepare for my exams without any doubts.

I went into the exam room with God and came out winning. I passed all my exams, and I was a part of the graduation listing. My mother was so happy. She talked about it every day. Her daily struggles weren't wasted. In that same year, I was matriculated to sixth form. I knew God was on my side. Going to sixth form was a privilege, and I knew I had to be settled. Of course, it was another beginning, and I had to think wisely and differently. That new stage brought new challenges. I now had to think about university, and I knew that my family wasn't in a position to pay college tuition. I tried to take one step at a time, but it was hard. *"I can't handle it,"* I said subconsciously, not knowing that most of what happens to us is how we speak to ourselves.

Most assignments were internet-based, and I had no personal computer. I either had to go to the library or visit my friend on the weekends. I visited my friend so often you would think I lived there. The greatest thing, though, was when I went there, it was just happy faces, so I knew I was always welcomed. I always knew that on my journey to success, I could never do it alone. I needed cooperation from others. With the help of my friend, I managed to finish my assignments and school-based assessments. Thank you, Cecilia, for all that you did.

The time had narrowed down, and I heard nothing from my father. I prayed that I would hear something from him because that would be my greatest joy. The pressure would be lifted from my mother's shoulder. The situation frustrated me because while others contemplated which university they would apply to, I had to keep quiet. I wasn't comfortable. I knew where I was from, and I didn't want to settle, but I had no other option. The hatred I had once lost for my father wanted to rekindle, but I didn't allow it, because I knew that being bitter would get me nowhere.

The time came, and while all my friends went off to university, I had to stay home. I still had faith, though my heart was saddened.

Were all my accomplishments for nothing?

CHAPTER 3

Bitten but Not Beaten

All my life had been to hell and back and being out of school and looking forward to nothingness made me wake up every day with regret and remorse. I wished that my mother had given me up for adoption when I was much younger. Maybe things would have been better. I didn't want to be where I was.

I continued praying, but I became very doubtful with every word that came out of my mouth. *How could God have done this to me? Why me, God? God knew all that I had been through, and He really chose to leave me like this?* Those were questions I continuously asked myself and God while looking in the mirror every minute of the day. Furthermore, with all those bizarre questions came pressure from my stepfather. He wanted me to step out of my comfort zone. *How could I move when my mind, soul, and feet were literally tired?* I was tired of praying and nothing happening. I really thought that prayer changes everything. I gave up on God! Faith! Hope!

I was heartbroken because my dreams were hindered. The weirdest thing was that my heart still worked after all that pressure. It still kept on pumping blood even when I didn't want it to. Each night, I sank into darkness, but I still woke up the next morning. I still saw the morning light and beautiful flowers and heard the voices of people moving around.

I was still alive!

Maybe I was still alive for a reason. Sink or swim? Nevertheless, I had to swim. I knew I couldn't live like that. I was grown, so I had to make a step. I had been through worse. My mother couldn't do it for me. I had to do it on my own.

I started writing motivational quotes on the wall. At that pivotal point, I came in contact with the most inspirational speaker of all time, Thomas Dexter Jakes, who boosted my faith. This time when I looked in the mirror, I spoke to myself in another way, *"This is not you. You are better than this. Your circumstances don't define who you are..."*

I looked at my life as being an investor. I wasn't a new investor because I had been doing business with God for a long time. He had blessed me on my rough and good days. Therefore, I looked at myself as an old investor because as a new investor, you panic when business is not going well, but old investors are different. They know that fluctuations will come, and it will help them to grow and ride out their storms. Old business owners know that the business will rise again. My problem was not about God, and it was not about my seed; my mustard seed that I planted. It was definitely about my soil.

I had to make a change and step out into an environment of possibilities.

A couple weeks passed, and I decided to volunteer at Windsor Primary School. I decided to seek a better job that could help me. I was definitely settling for mediocrity, but I did it anyway. I had to start somewhere. I started serving in September 2015. However, knowing I wasn't being paid was one of the hardest things to deal with. Bills were to be paid at home, and I had college to think about in the upcoming year. The greatest thing about it was I had the resilience and the tenacity to never give up despite my many adversities.

I was never comfortable with settling.

Luckily, I met a great individual at the institution who was there for me through thick and thin. Her name was Ms. Parsons, a very sturdy and courteous young lady. She cared about my well-being. She was my mentor. I could talk to her about anything.

I knew she saw something in me when she said, *"Cherish, don't settle here. Have big dreams and always push yourself out of your comfort zone."*

She made me believe in myself again, even when I didn't want to.

My worries about not being paid ended one morning when my brother's friend showed up, neatly tucked in black pants and a rose-pink shirt, asking the principal for a recommendation. He was attending a meeting for the appointment of teacher assistants. I was advised by the principal to accompany him to see if I was lucky enough to be appointed. I thought that was quite odd, but I went anyway. When I turned up, I wasn't accounted for. However, I chose to stay throughout the meeting to see if there was another opportunity. For the entire meeting, I was distraught because all eyes were on me. I could imagine their revolting thoughts, *"Who is she?"* or *"She is so inquisitive,"* which I was for showing up at a meeting that I wasn't invited to.

After the meeting, the coordinator told me that they couldn't accommodate me as a teacher assistant. I was devastated. Later, I went home and cried to God because I needed that job. I prayed a prayer that moved God because when I was through, I was filled with sweat and my voice was almost gone. But how could I be praying about something that I already got a "no" to? Well, I did because I never underestimated my God. It was an issue of faith, and I had faith that I would hear a yes.

A couple days passed, and I was sitting in grade one assisting Ms. Parsons when a student told me that the principal had called me into her office. She was a huge lady with a big voice and big hands. Just the thought of that made me quiver because I was wondering what the problem was. When I arrived, she chuckled and said, *"You are so blessed! Did you know that the coordinator for the teacher assistant program just called and filled you in?"*

I was dumbfounded. I knew that God was good, but that must have been a miracle. He comes through all the time, and I was elated. I knew I had to be in church the following Sunday.

I was supposed to start working on October 5, 2015. When I went home that evening, I had to pray and thank God for what He was doing for me. I was so grateful. It happened because I didn't give up on God. It was the will of FAITH and PRAYER. When God says YES, no man can say NO. I could now start planning for college and help to pay the bills at home.

BUT! Optimism turned into pessimism quickly in months. I forgot about my real plans. I started partying recklessly, buying unnecessary things, and worst of all, I fell in love. It was my broken heart that led me back to reality. After numerous outings with my partner and spending time with him, I realized that I was living a life of lies. My partner had somebody else all along and didn't tell me about it. That left my heart sore. Again, another man broke my heart, and I didn't know how to handle it. I cried like a baby. Those were the times I wished I was a child to just crawl into the arms of my mother and cry my eyes out. I went weeks without eating or sleeping. I knew broken crayons still color, so I had to keep it moving because my father did me worst.

It was in June 2016 when my working contract was about to end that I regained consciousness. It was too late. I had wasted almost a year, and I didn't know how to get back on my feet.

Another September arrived, and I was back in the same position. It seemed I had a pathology for returning to the same places. I couldn't allow myself to be happy because it was entirely my fault. I was in a mess. I woke up every morning knowing what my routine was like, and I definitely got bored. I let go of God's hands, so I started to fail. I could hear my mother's voice in my head: *"When you get the blessing and forget the Blesser, you are bound to fail,"* and I did.

However, to avoid the frustration and the combustion between my stepfather and me, I went back to volunteering. I felt as if my stepfather couldn't stand to see me anymore. At least, that was what I thought. *How could someone who had so much love for me and played the role of my father have so much hatred for me?* The thought brought me to tears. Still, I had to mature as a person and know that what he wanted was for me to PUSH and rise from my situation.

Returning to volunteerism was settling for average. It wasn't me! I knew I had the potential. What was I doing? I was supposed to be in school.

Weeks went by. No help, boring days, sleepless nights, and no calls for an interview. I couldn't give up. Often, images flashed across my eyes of when I was on the market truck with my mother, and it brought me to tears because I promised her that things would get better and they weren't. Each morning, I dragged myself out of bed with great compunction. I volunteered for the entirety of 2016. Who does that? I often compared myself to my other colleagues who were in university, and that made it even worse.

I still held on to faith, and I never stopped praying, especially about my father. He was now in a better position to help me, and I wanted his help. My prayers worked, and we started communicating. I didn't know where I found the strength to talk to him, but I did. It was just God. He had built me in such a way that I forgot the past because holding on to my past only made me bitter. Forgiveness is a blessing. When you pray, forgive, and forget, you make yourself free, and you have a lot more capacity to receive. I spoke with my father about having no job, and he decided to help me get a visa to travel overseas to where he was, so I could have a life there. It was truly faith that brought us together.

On December 13, 2016 at approximately 8:00 a.m., I was standing in line at the United States Embassy in Kingston. While getting a visa wasn't a big deal for most people, it was for me. I had great plans. It was going to be a big step for me because that way things would be better for me and my family. I had so much faith.

Little did I know that I was setting myself up for failure. I received the biggest turn down of my life. I was denied the visa, and the major problem was to face my mother. She was the one who accompanied me. I stood inside the embassy with disbelief, making plans to find another route to go outside and face her. Oh God! I knew I had failed her. I pushed the door open to greet my mother, and I could no longer hold the tears. I was devastated! Not only because I was denied, but the tears of my mother touched every organ inside my body. I was haunted by that moment, and I decided to use it as a stepping stone. Wherever I go and whatever I do, I will never forget December 13, the day I saw my mother cry her hardest.

I went home smiling because I was trying to hide the tears. I had to keep the faith and continually hold on to God's hand, even when things weren't going my way, even though it was hard. My sister soothed me when she said, *"Everything in life happens for a reason."* She encouraged me to continue to pray and fast. I could feel my life changing because I was now building a prayer life. I was in the same position but felt my life changing.

With that feeling, I started re-applying for schools locally and internationally.

When the next term arrived, I knew I had to volunteer, but my mindset was different. I still had burdens, and I still cried tears, but I had a prayer life, and prayer changes everything. It was hard boosting my faith again after all I had been through, but I had to BELIEVE. I couldn't trust the emblems of my past to determine the emblems of my future. I had to look at life from the perspective that the good outweighs the bad.

Often, I reflected on what life was like, and I knew that great things were ahead because once upon a time, I prayed for something better. I was going through hell, but I was smiling. I embraced my darkness, knowing that a light is always at the end of the tunnel. My mindset was different. I carried faith in my arms like a baby. I sought the good in everything I did. I worked with instincts. I became an optimist.

Finally, I received some good news. In February 2017, I was accepted to the University of the West Indies and the University of Technology locally, and Bethune Cookman and Barry University internationally. I didn't know where I was going to get the money, but I knew God would help me because He was always on my side. My outlook on life made things better because I knew that a whole new attitude or outlook could change the situation. I was elated.

In order to attend school abroad, I had to take the SATs. I didn't know where to find the first cent, but I asked Ms. Parsons, and she agreed to help me. I believe that sometimes God positions people in situations to help you because He knows that when you get there, you are going to need help. The SATs were paid for, and I applied to the Student Loan Bureau. God is good.

No matter how well things are going, the devil always wants to snatch it away. I had to learn the hard way that not everything was meant to be, and sometimes God does test our faith. Bethune refused my application. I had no bank letter to show that I could afford my studies abroad. I wanted to give up, but I had my eyes on the prize. I was determined to attend college to become a teacher. I couldn't give up.

My only work shoes had deteriorated, and a company was hounding me for payments regarding my computer. Still, in the midst of all that was happening, I had to trust God, and I had the support of my cousin, Suzanne, telling me to never give in. I continued to pray.

My prayer worked, and things turned around. My transcript was paid for, and a friend of mine told me about Daytona State College. Ms. Parsons paid the application fee, and I took my SATs. I was offered a National Youth Service job through which I met a lot of dignitaries who I knew God was going to use to shape my future. Unfortunately, the job was only for one month.

Months went by, and I heard nothing from Daytona State College until one day they emailed me about another bank letter. I panicked for a moment, and then I decided to contact people who I thought could help me. I wasn't about to doubt God again because I knew that He could help me with that one. I contacted a few people directly and indirectly, and most of them said yes, and I was grateful. However, weeks went by, and nothing happened. Each yes had turned to no. Doors were shut in my face.

One morning, I woke up to a message that, surprisingly, gave me hope. It read, *"Good morning. I really wanted to help, but I am afraid signing an affidavit is too much to ask. I am truly sorry, and I hope that things will work out. Keep praying; the Lord will come through for you."*

The last part of the message restored my faith: *"Keep praying; the Lord will come through for you,"* and that was exactly what I did. My fervent prayers were answered in December 2017 when my stepfather's father decided to help me out. Additionally, my father was willing to help me out again with the interview process. I was extremely grateful. I could no longer deny that God was amazing and never too busy to help anyone out in any situation.

When the New Year came, I was in church worshipping. I had to give God thanks. I could tell that the year approaching was going to be a great one.

On January 5, 2018 I was told that I had mail. I collected it and came home to open it. I was really happy and nervous at the same time. Tendrils of ice spread throughout my body, wrapping around my spine and curling up in my gut while I lazily opened the letter.

It started with the following words, "*Congratulations Cherish...*" and I could no longer bring myself to read the rest of the letter. I stood there in disbelief while tears fell from my eyes. I threw my hands up in exasperation and all I could say was, 'Thank You Jesus."

God doesn't fail. He may be late, but He is always on time. I sensed there was a new beginning or there was a new mountain to climb. Maybe there were hurdles, new challenges, or another story. All I knew was that I held on and I will forever hold on to my Mustard Seed Faith.

A Letter to My Readers

I meticulously wrote this book to let my readers know that whatever happens in life, you should not lose your hold on two main ropes–hope and faith. Those who have faith, have hope; and those who have hope, have faith.

On your life's journey, there will be losses, heartbreaks, struggles, and even failures. There will be moments when you doubt yourself or spend days on your knees asking God, *"Why me?"* Those are tough times, but the tough times have not come to stay; they have come to pass.

I have been through a lot of struggles, mainly with transitioning to university. I consider myself a victor today because I am now a student at the University of the West Indies *open* Campus and I am the proud President of the Fueled By Faith Charity Initiative. I have much further to go and this has all happened because I held on to God's hands and walked by faith. I am not perfect because I was a pessimist. I doubted God a lot, and I was apprehensive whenever I reached pivotal points in my life. However, the words of my mentor, *"Worries solve nothing; pray about everything,"* gave me hope and helped me to develop a prayer life. Consequently, having a prayer life and walking with faith as my light, guided me while I was walking through my tunnel.

I would encourage my readers to have a mind to build, never give in, and don't give up on your dreams. Right now, you might be in a situation that you think you won't survive. However, six months ago, or two years ago, you may have been in a situation you didn't think you would survive either. The point is, you will always surprise yourself, and you will always make it through. You are alive, so you are still in the race.

Walk out your journey of faith!

You can't read a book about prayer and see results. It is what God takes you through that will make you pray and develop an effective prayer life.

Conclusion

No matter how great you are, you can never know your destiny, or where you are going, unless you have faith.

In the same way that everyone must live and learn, so it is for the young, God-fearing, Cherish Walker; an individual who encountered many trials, struggles, and obstacles on the journey to success but used faith and endurance to conquer it all.

> *"But let patience have her perfect work, that ye may be perfect and entire, wanting nothing."*
>
> James 1:4

When You Need Motivation

~ *"If you knew who your God was; you would stop running away from your devils."*

– T. D. Jakes

~ *Your attitude determines your altitude.*

~ *"God's plan to bless you may not come with a support system. It may be controversial, and the only way to sustain yourself may be to find someone who has been there too."*

– T. D. Jakes

~ *Focus on where you want to go, not where you currently are.*

~ *BELIEVE!*

~ *"Success is not where you are in life, but the obstacles you have overcome."*

– Booker T. Washington

~ *"Some men have thousands of reasons why they cannot do what they want to; all they need is one reason why they can."*

– Willis Whitney

~ *Remember, if you want a different result, do something different.*

~ *Take a risk – jump out of your comfort zone.*

~ *Don't let self-doubt hold you back.*

`~ *"Commit yourself to a dream. Nobody who tries to do something great, but fails, is a total failure. Why? Because he can always be assured that he succeeded in life's most important battle; he defeated the battle of not trying."*

–Robert H. Schuller

~ *"Most of our obstacles would melt away if, instead of cowering before them, we should make up our minds to walk boldly through them."*

– Orison Swett Marden

~ *"Twenty years from now, you'd be more disappointed by the things you didn't do, then by the things you did do. So throw off the bowlines! Sail away from the safe harbour. Catch the trade winds in your sails. Explore, dream, and discover."*

– Mark Twain

~ *"To move the world, we must first move ourselves."*

– Socrates

~ *Winning starts with beginning.*

~ *If opportunity doesn't knock, build a door.*

~ *"You may have a fresh start at any moment you choose, for this thing we call 'failure' is not falling down, but staying down."*

–Mary Pickford

~ *"Step by step. I can't think of any other way of accomplishing anything."*

–Michael Jordan

~ *"To win, you have to risk loss."*

–Jean Claude Killy

~ *Once you learn to quit, it becomes a habit.*

~ *Hebrews 11:1: "Now faith is the substance of things hoped for, the evidence of things not seen."*

~ *"When you get into a tight place and everything goes against you, until it seems as though you could not hang on a minute longer, it is then when you should never give up, for that is just the place and time when the tide will turn."*

– Harriet Beecher Stowe

~ *"If you are not happy every morning when you get up, leave for work, or start to work at home, and are not enthusiastic about doing that, you will not be successful."*

– Donald M. Kendall

~ What is fear? F= false, E= evidence, A= appearing, R= real. Don't be afraid of any false evidence and just do it.

~ "Nothing can take the place of persistence. Talent will not; nothing is more common than unsuccessful men with talent. Genius will not; unrewarded genius is almost a proverb. Education will not; the world is full of educated derelicts. Persistence and determination alone are omnipotent."

–Calvin Coolidge

"Never give up on what you really want to do. The person with big dreams is more powerful than the one with all of the facts."

– Life's Little Instruction Book

~ "One day you'll be in a room filled with your ancestors; don't be the one who contributed to nothing."

– J. Wesley

"To those of you with your years of service still ahead, the challenge is yours. Stop doubting yourselves. Have the courage to make up your mind and hold your decisions."

– Dr. Mary Bethune,
Founder of Bethune Cookman University

Matthew 13: 31-32: *"Another parable put he forth unto them, saying, The kingdom of heaven is like to a grain of mustard seed, which a man took, and sowed in his field: Which indeed is the least of all seeds: but when it is grown, it is the greatest among herbs, and becometh a tree, so that the birds of the air come and lodge in the branches thereof."*

Famous Motivational Stories

Elephant Rope

A gentleman was walking through an elephant camp, and he noticed that the elephants weren't being kept in cages or held by the use of chains. All that was holding them back from escaping the camp was a small piece of rope tied to one of their legs.

As the man gazed upon the elephants, he was completely confused as to why the elephants didn't just use their strength to break the rope and escape the camp. They could easily have done so, but instead, they didn't try to at all.

Curious and wanting to know the answer, he asked a trainer nearby why the elephants were just standing there and never tried to escape.

The trainer replied, *"When they are very young and much smaller, we use the same size rope to tie them and, at that age, it's enough to hold them. As they grow up, they are conditioned to believe that they cannot break away. They believe the rope can still hold them, so they never try to break free."*

The only reason the elephants weren't breaking free and escaping from the camp was that over time, they adopted the belief that it just wasn't possible.

Moral of the story: No matter how much the world tries to hold you back, always continue with the belief and faith that what you want to achieve is possible. Believing you can become successful is the most important step in actually achieving it.

Lulu Roman's Story

Lulu's struggle started the day she was born in a home of unwed mothers. At age four, she was dropped off at an orphanage, where she was raised. She was a fat child, and she struggled with thyroid dysfunction. She was taunted with cruel songs such as: *"Fatty, fatty, 2 by 4; can't get through the kitchen door."* She often wished for a family to take her, but none did.

They didn't adopt fat kids.

She stayed at the orphanage until she was 18. Lulu wanted a normal life, but she didn't have one, so she resorted to her God-given talent for humor to cope. With this talent, she soon became a star when she met Carol Burnett in Hollywood.

With being a star, consequences came, and soon Lulu had discovered drugs. She lost her spot and found out that she was pregnant and alone. She was married, but she blamed God for her spouse dumping her. Furthermore, her drug habit worsened because she had no one to care for her and she didn't care for herself. As a result, her son came into the world with the same habits. She got news that he was going to die, so she resorted to praying. Unfortunately, she didn't know how to pray.

"Yo, dude, if you save my son, I will straighten my life."

The doctor made it clear that only God could help her son, and God did just that. On the medical card, it read, *"An act of God."*

However, years passed, and she forgot her promise, so God sent a messenger. While leaving jail for drug possession arrest, Lulu ran into Diane. Diane was her friend from the orphanage. This was a divine intervention. Because of the communication with Diane about Jesus, she gave her life to the Lord. She was miraculously healed from drug addiction.

Producers invited her back to *Hee Haw's* comedy, but before she went, she did something that she hadn't done in past years – she prayed.

She dedicated her life to sharing her testimony of how God's grace changed her life. She recorded gospel albums and gave to orphans. She said, *"I know I can't gather up a ton of these kids and adopt them and take care of them, but I can make them laugh for a little while. I can take them to great places and take their minds off feeling sad. And that's what I want to do."*

How awesome is our God?

The Obstacle in Our Path

In ancient times, a king had a boulder placed on a roadway. He then hid himself and watched to see if anyone would move the boulder out of the way. Some of the king's wealthiest merchants and courtiers came by and simply walked around it.

Many people loudly blamed the king for not keeping the roads clear, but none of them did anything about getting the stone out of the way.

A peasant then came along carrying a load of vegetables. Upon approaching the boulder, the peasant laid down his burden and tried to push the stone out of the road. After much pushing and straining, he finally succeeded.

After the peasant went back to pick up his vegetables, he noticed a purse lying in the road where the boulder had been. The purse contained many gold coins and a note from the king explaining that the gold was for the person who removed the boulder from the roadway.

Moral of the story: Every obstacle we come across in life gives us an opportunity to improve our circumstances, and while the lazy complain, others are creating opportunities through their kind hearts, generosity, and willingness to get things done.

Dedication to Mama

Having a child doesn't make you a mother. It takes a lifetime to be a good mother. While the child is growing, the mother is growing, and it is at that point of growth where the bonding begins. Mothers are the foundation and the core of whatever you are building. For whatever you encounter in this life, you are going to need a mother's advice.

This book is dedicated to the woman who kept me through my dark times, the one person who will never give up on me, my mother, Miss Sharon Clarke.

My mother is a woman of honor. She is a phenomenal, resilient, God-fearing, and generous woman. I love her from the very bottom of my heart.

I want to tell her thanks for:

1. Teaching us to pray
2. Teaching us how to be patient

3. Teaching us to be responsible
4. Teaching us to love ourselves
5. Teaching us to endure

And most of all:

THANK YOU FOR MOULDING US.

When I look at this crazy world today, I have to be grateful for the moulding and I will never defer from it.

Mama, thank you for teaching us to BELIEVE! You taught me to believe in myself before I believe in anything else and that was, and still is, my favourite lesson that you taught us.

God has given me the best mother of all and for all times. I would never replace her for anything. I would go miles for her, and I would give up my life for her. Many would think I am crazy, but these are the things you do for somebody you love.

When she found out she was pregnant with me as her third child, she could have easily aborted me. When I came into this world, she could have given me up for adoption, but she didn't, even though life was hard, she kept it together. I thank you, Mama.

She has endured a lot, and I gave her heartaches upon heartaches, but she didn't give up on me or the rest of us. She kept us close, she prayed for and with us. Here I am today, smiling, knowing that we have made you proud. It might not be major, but as you always say, *"It is the little things."*

When I told her about this book, she laughed and said, *"Tressan, you are rich already, and you haven't even started. You are always making me proud."* You are always making me smile and encouraging me in subtle ways and that is all I need in this life.

Miss Sharon, thank you for believing in me even when I didn't believe in myself and for praying for me when I couldn't. I am proud to call you mother.

I appreciate you so much, Ma.

www.ingramcontent.com/pod-product-compliance
Lightning Source LLC
Chambersburg PA
CBHW070106100426
42743CB00012B/2662